CONFESSIONS
OF A SECTION 8
LANDLORD

By Sara Aviles

Copyright © 2023 Sara Aviles
All rights reserved.

All rights reserved. No part of this publication may be reproduced, distributed, or transmitted in any form or by any means, including photocopying, recording, or other electronic or mechanical methods, without the prior written permission of the author. Reproduction or translation of this work in any form beyond that permitted by section 107 or 108 of the 1976 United States Copyright Act is strictly prohibited. For permission requests, please contact the author.

Limit of Liability/Disclaimer of Warranty: This book is intended for entertainment purposes only. The contents of this book are provided on an "as is" basis, and we make no representations or warranties of any kind, express or implied, with respect to the accuracy or completeness of the contents of this book. The information contained within this book is not intended to replace or serve as a substitute for professional advice. Furthermore, all names of individuals mentioned in this book have been changed to protect their privacy and confidentiality. In no event shall the authors or publishers be liable for any direct, indirect, incidental, special, or consequential damages arising out of or in any way connected with the use or inability to use this book. All references in this book are for information purposes only and are not warranted for content, accuracy, or any other implied or explicit purpose. By reading this book, you agree to release and hold harmless the author and publisher from any and all claims, damages, or other liabilities arising from or in connection with the use of this book.

Paperback ISBN: 978-1-66640-212-4
eBook ISBN: 978-1-66640-213-1

Table of Contents

The Beginning of the End 4

Bundle of Lies 13

Case of the Disappearing Manager 17

The "Unhandy" Handywoman 24

The Corrupt Politician 34

The Hand-Me-Down Unit 39

The Handsy Handyman 42

The Scam Artist 45

Subsidized Housing – The Good, The Bad, and The Ugly 50

Robin Hood of the Street 57

Attack of the Roaches 60

The Gentle Giant 66

Electrical Russian Roulette 72

The Dreaded Slip and Fall 76

Selling the Unsellable 81

Failing Up 86

Epilogue – Giving Back 95

Sources 107

The Beginning of the End

"What am I doing?!" I thought as I worked around the clock dealing with squatters, reports of tenants setting up swimming pools in their units, as well as trying to keep the local drug lord at bay from using our apartment building as a trap house. I was at my wit's end after self-managing a 12-unit apartment complex in one of the most dangerous cities in the United States. With a population of roughly 320,000 people, this city had almost 40 homicides in one year. Most of those homicides happened within a one-mile radius of our property.

Let me start by giving you some background information about myself. I have always been obsessed with real estate. I take that back. I became obsessed with real estate after taking a required college class on "How to Manage a Household". Initially, I thought it was going to be a complete waste of my time. However, little did I know it would change my life. The instructor was not what I imagined. He was funny, had a very successful career, and this was the only class he taught. The one key thing I took away was that in order to make long-term sound financial decisions, you have to invest. His investment of choice was real estate. He introduced me to Robert Kiyosaki's book, "Rich Dad Poor Dad", [1] and after that, I was hooked. I fell in love with the dream of being "out of the rat race" as he called it, and started to list measurable goals to figure out how long it would take me to become "financially free". I mean, what 20-year-old doesn't want to retire early on passive income? So, I set my sights on the future and put all my time, money, and energy into making this dream become a reality.

I devoured book after book on real estate and saved every dollar I had for my first down payment. While other students were eating out, I was counting every dollar to get to my goal. By the time I graduated college at the age of 21, I was able to just barely afford my first property. It was a small single-family home that had recently been ripped back to the studs and completely renovated. My boyfriend—now husband—and I moved in straight out of college, putting only $16,000 down, with plans to rent it out after we could afford to purchase our second property. The payment was all I could afford but the risk paid off in spades.

In a few years, we were able to get our second home. This time and every time since I purchased a property, I would be filled with dread so palatable that it would make me nauseous. It was as if I was about to run full speed off a cliff. However, I knew that the risk would be worth the reward. After we moved, we were strapped again with little funds, having to be able to qualify for two mortgages in order to make the move. Being that the new house was less than 30 minutes away, we were able to self-manage our first rental with little to no problems. Everything ran smoothly. Our previous home was completely renovated when we purchased it, so there was no deferred maintenance to worry about. We were also fortunate enough to have had the same great tenants for over four years.

A few years later, burned out from a high-stress sales job and struggling to make ends meet after the arrival of our baby boy, we decided we needed a reset. I had a burning desire to stay home and raise my son. Not to mention the daycare options that I could afford were less than stellar. Taking drastic measures, we sold both our properties and moved in with my in-laws. In my mind, this was the epitome of failure. I mean, what 28-year-old wants to move in with their parents? Or in my case, my in-laws. While it was a painful decision, looking back, it really helped propel us forward in our investing career and gave me the ability to raise my son. Plus, it surprisingly strengthened my relationship with my mother-in-law.

Confessions of a Section 8 Landlord

Timing the market well, we sold our initial investment property for almost double the original purchase price. Doing a 1031 exchange, which is a tool that allows you to defer payment of capital gains, we were able to preserve our profits and trade up into a 12-unit apartment complex. We had looked at other cities, but all the cap rates were 5% or lower, which wasn't exciting for us. For those of you that are unfamiliar with real estate terminology, a cap rate is the ratio between the annual net operating income produced by the property and its market value. If you were not leveraging the property with a loan, the cap rate would be your rate of return on the property. One day, I saw one with a 9% cap rate. Excited, I showed my husband, and we made an offer that day. Being in our 20s and having bounds of unearned confidence, we took on the project of purchasing our first apartment complex with a hefty six-hour commute. I mean, how hard can it be, right? If you are a seasoned investor, you are already laughing. Just wait… it gets better.

Our first investment went so well that we didn't think much about the area we were purchasing in. As long as we held the property long enough, we would be golden. My aunt and uncle had a small single-family home in a nicer part of the city that they had rented out for over 15 years with little to no problems. We didn't think to look up the stability of the city at the time. If we did, we would have found that the city had recently gone bankrupt (which means sky-high property taxes, yikes!). When we did our inspection of the 12-unit apartment building, it was a beautiful day. We had eaten lunch at an amazing hipster restaurant that served avocado toast to die for, and the city seemed respectable. That was an anomaly. We ended up buying a property not only in one of the most dangerous cities in the United States, but in the worst four blocks of that city.

Even insurance companies wouldn't take this building. As we received one denied insurance application after another, we assumed that it was just harder to get insurance for an apartment building. In the end, we ended up going with the current insurance carrier, which was the only insurance provider that would insure that building. Obviously, the insurance companies knew more than we did. The street the property was on was known for police officers getting shot on it, parades for drug lords, and for "ghetto taking care of ghetto" as one of our tenants called it. We were in for a crazy ride as we managed a solid F class property right as the Covid-19 pandemic hit the nation.

If that wasn't deterrent enough, you know you have a rotten apple when all the reputable property management companies refuse to manage it. One after another, they would look up the address and kindly say, "This isn't the right fit for us," with no explanation. Or another one of my favorites, "You know what you purchased, right?" We had to all but beg a management company to take our money and look after this building. Not that it did us much good. As soon as Covid hit, our property management company ceased all management activities—besides collecting rent and their paycheck. This left us to try and manage the most difficult properties we will have ever encountered in our investing career during one of the most challenging times in history. All from over six hours away.

This book is a collection of stories we compiled over the last two and a half years while we owned the building. It is common when meeting with other investors to share your battle stories. "What is the worst building you ever bought?" they would ask, and man would I have a story for them. If I did not completely scare them off after they heard the tales of my tenants' outlandish ways to save on rent, run-ins with the local gang leaders, and multiple squatters, I knew they were going to have the guts to make it big. I am writing this in hopes that you not only learn from our mistakes, but maybe get some joy out of another investor's pain that just might be a little worse than the headache you are currently enduring. This book is not meant to put you off investing, as I have found investing in low-income housing to be one of the most rewarding things I have done.

However, it does shed some light on some of the pitfalls you might discover when dealing with some of these types of properties.

While I initially wrote this book as my own cathartic way of processing everything we went through while managing this building, it has developed into a story that I hope both my fellow investors and housing advocates will read. During the process of writing this book, I have been working with various housing advocacy groups to work on fixing the lack of housing available for the unhoused and create better pathways to permanent housing solutions. While I know my story is very one-sided, and there is much that needs to be changed in the real estate industry, I wrote this in hopes that we can see that there are a lot of shades of gray when it comes to housing issues. When we are able to start an open, honest dialogue between these two very polarized sides, we can start the hard work to find win-win solutions that bring landlords and housing advocates together.

Warning, this book sheds light on a lot of the moral dilemmas small investors faced during the eviction moratorium. While we like to see things in black and white, during this time when our hands were tied and thousands of investors were losing their life savings, we had to work in the gray. Keeping hardworking, honest tenants in housing is a noble cause, which we wholeheartedly support. However, many took advantage of the situation. Not all these scenarios are going to fit nicely in a box of what you may think is good or bad. If you are easily offended by these issues, this might not be the book for you. However, I urge you to keep an open mind and consider what you would do if you were responsible for these 12 units, as well as supporting a family of your own.

To give you some insight on my background, I grew up in the Bay Area of California, which I later found was called "the liberal safe haven" by other investors. Growing up in a very left-leaning community and being raised by a mother who was the director of a nonprofit supporting the unhoused, I knew being a landlord was not looked kindly upon. I thought I was well-versed in the struggles of low-income communities. I even referred to the St Vincent De Paul soup kitchen as my second home, where I spent many hours volunteering there alongside my mother. My brother and I had a second family there as a group of the guests looked at us as their honorary children. You would find us most weekends playing checkers with the guests or stocking the pantries after school. Little did I know, I was still very sheltered from many harsh realities. You truly do not know the struggles that both low-income tenants and small independent landlords face until you are in the thick of it.

Confessions of a Section 8 Landlord

You hear over-dramatized horror stories on the news of these evil landlords. However, they don't show you both sides as that would not sell papers. My mother changed many of her viewpoints after hearing of my struggles while managing this building. She was my go-to person whenever I was trying to help one of our low-income tenants. Even with her immense amount of experience in public service, working with the unhoused for more than 14 years and low-income youth for 40 years, some of these situations still stumped her. She saw us first-hand struggling to come up with numerous solutions that kept my tenants' best interests in mind while trying not to lose the building to the bank.

It is easy to vilify someone you don't know. However, when you hear stories from someone you know is a well-intentioned person, struggling to make the best decision, there is a paradigm shift. While I do not like to discuss politics, I firmly believe when we are able to have honest open discussions about some of these issues on both sides is where we see lasting change. With that, I will let you decide.

Bundle of Lies

When we first purchased the apartment building, we were ecstatic. The building looked to be completely renovated and in solid condition. The previous owner had bought the building vacant at a local auction with the plans to flip it. Knowing the importance of professional property inspections, we paid top dollar for an in-depth inspection of the apartment complex. The building looked like it was in pristine condition for the age of the property. However, this was a quick flip and not much thought went into the plumbing and electrics. When we had to do electrical work and investigated behind the facade, we were dismayed to find shoddy electrical work hidden behind the drywall. It was not disclosed at the time that our building inspector was also a close friend of the owner. Not only that, but since they were flipping the apartment complex, they didn't worry about thoroughly screening their tenants. They just filled it with bodies and sold it. Which gives you some insight on the quality of tenants we inherited.

Confessions of a Section 8 Landlord

As soon as the purchase was complete, we started unraveling some of the lies we were told in escrow. The property was marketed at a 9% cap rate, which is the net income divided by the property value. That number was calculated incorrectly, and we later found it would be closer to a 6%-7% cap rate. That's okay, we thought it was still better than the cap rates we were seeing elsewhere. When we were speaking with the owner directly, he gave us some feedback that simply was not true. Worried about the status of the Section 8 tenants, we inquired if all were currently up to date with their rent. The owner informed us that all tenants were up to date and not to worry about having to evict Section 8 tenants as Section 8 would handle the eviction. For those of you that have worked with Section 8 tenants, you know that is completely inaccurate. While the tenants would lose their Section 8 voucher upon being evicted, the landlord is solely responsible for taking care of the eviction proceedings.

"What about your real estate agent?" some have asked me. "Where were they when all of this was happening?" Like many new investors, we used a friend who was a residential real estate agent as we did not know there was a difference between a commercial and residential real estate agent at the time. Our agent had the best of intentions but didn't know much more than we did about commercial real estate. Because of this, we ended up negotiating with the owner of the building directly. Being young and naïve, we took the building owner for his word. Not only was he giving us a false sense of security, but we found out that not all of the tenants were paying. One of the tenants stopped paying rent two months into their lease, and a couple more were behind on their payments. Looking back, I should have requested estoppel certificates signed off by all the tenants and the landlord, which would be a legally binding written verification of the terms, conditions, and status of the leases they had signed off on. However, at that time, both my residential agent and I didn't know what an estoppel was, let alone to request one.

Well, at least we have the guaranteed subsidized payment to get us through the transition period, we thought. Unfortunately, Section 8 took about three months to transfer the subsidized payment to us. This left us to float the loan payments until we could get this corrected. During this time, the previous owner continued to receive Section 8 payments, cashed them, and did not inform us. We had to harass his office for weeks until he finally agreed to give us the payments as well as some security deposits he kept hidden from us.

We had found out the truth of what was going on from his on-site building manager, Kalisha, who we decided to keep on during the ownership transition. Kalisha lived in unit one and had some unique management choices. Rather than taking on the task of mopping and keeping the hallways free of debris, Kalisha had the tenants on rotating cleaning shifts. We heard about this from one of our tenants, who complained that she was worried about getting evicted for not being able to clean due to a health condition. We immediately hired a professional cleaning crew and let Kalisha know this practice was a huge liability.

Another difficulty we didn't foresee is Kalisha, like most of our tenants, didn't own a printer. So, every time we needed something posted, she would have to go to Kinkos and pay their exorbitant rates. She would send us pictures of the receipts with her long purple talon nails in every frame. I remember printing out documents and mailing them to her, which was a much simpler process than the multiple calls it took to get through the Kinkos process. Kalisha also handled all the accounting up until this point. This consisted of her writing down the rent, barely legible and sideways, on scratch paper and sending me a photo. Needless to say, we quickly transitioned to a professional property management company.

Case of the Disappearing Manager

We had owned our first apartment building for a little shy of a year before the Covid-19 outbreak. During that time, the building was professionally managed, and while we had some headaches, we had done a good job of dialing everything in. In the fall before the pandemic took the nation by surprise, we decided to hire a new property manager that was highly recommended. There are always growing pains when transitioning property managers, however, it started out exceedingly well. The management team had clean, understandable accounting software, were great with the tenants, and had a long-term vision for the property. That all changed shortly after January 2020, as our world turned upside down.

While we had many road bumps in the first year of owning our apartment complex, the real fun began when Covid changed our world as we know it. We didn't think much of it when the virus started to hit the news until our property manager stopped managing the building. They informed us that one of our tenants sneezed while they were on site, and after that, they refused to step foot in the apartment complex. They were worried that someone might be infected with the virus. While our property management team continued to collect rent, as well as our checks, they let the building become overrun with squatters and roaches. So, I did the only logical thing—I fired my property manager and managed the building myself during a worldwide pandemic. Did I mention I lived over six hours away! I mean, how hard can it be, right?

It seems I am getting ahead of myself. Before we let go of our management team, we had already started taking on the burden of many complicated situations that the property manager simply wouldn't do due to health and safety concerns, as well as the changing eviction policies. There was a vacant unit in our building that was in the process of being renovated. Turning a unit normally takes about 30 days in this market. However, this unit had been vacant for some time. Concerned about the little to no progress, I reached out to the property manager regarding this unit's status of being rented. I was informed that nothing had been renovated and it had, in fact, been sitting untouched for almost two months as her staff didn't feel comfortable going into the building due to Covid.

Confessions of a Section 8 Landlord

Not only was I losing out on potential rent that was keeping our building afloat, but to make matters worse, due to the lack of movement, we found ourselves with a squatter in unit six. This squatter had been there for 30 days and was running up a massive water bill. The squatter would leave her children unattended for long stretches of time, allowing them to wreak havoc on the building. Their main source of entertainment was the garden hose in our outdoor communal space. They would turn on the garden hose full blast and play in the water pools they would create.

After this experience, I understood why in the book, "Evicted: Poverty and Profit in the American City" by Matthew Desmond, [1] he disclosed that it is common practice not to rent units to low-income families with children. Many low-income families don't have access to childcare and will leave their children alone while they go to work. These children are left unattended with little to no toys, so, naturally, they find other ways to amuse themselves. They often spend their time seeing what things they can flush down the toilet, using the drapes as superhero capes, or in our case, turning our side garden into a marsh. I don't blame the kids—as a mother, I know first-hand the things my five-year-old son can get into after I leave him alone even just for a few minutes as I try to make dinner.

Confessions of a Section 8 Landlord

When we confronted our manager regarding this situation, she claimed she called the police three times but it took too long so she was forced to leave and get back to her other duties as we were not her only clients. Determined to solve the squatter situation, my husband made the six-hour drive to our property. First things first, he capped the exterior water line so there would be no more mud play ponds in the side yard. I mean, who needs plants anyways? Sympathizing for the women in our unit, my husband let her know that we would be willing to pay for a night in a hotel, help her move, give her some cash to relocate, as well as find her a place at a local shelter. Back in our hometown, I had made calls all day to make sure we had a place lined up for her that would take her and her children. The difficulty we found is that most shelters will not take someone who isn't sober. Knowing she was under the influence, finding a shelter that would take her and her kids was a much more daunting task. But after hours of phone calls, I was able to secure a place for them.

When my husband approached her with our solution, she started balling, saying she was from out of state and had nowhere to go. She went on to say she doesn't know anyone and was driving for Uber Eats before her car got towed. The big kicker is, she claimed the previous tenant gave her the keys and she paid them a deposit. Hearing all of this, my husband felt heartbroken for her and didn't know how he could morally remove her. That empathy quickly dissipated after he saw her leave the building dressed to the nines, leaving her two, six, and ten-year-old children alone in the apartment. We immediately called child protective services as these children were being left unattended in an unsafe environment. Unfortunately, child protection services were unable to intervene as there was no physical proof at the time of their arrival that she was leaving them unattended for hours, and only just helped further aggravate the situation. After multiple attempts to rehouse her, and the outright refusal to leave, we had to take more drastic measures.

First thing in the morning, my husband called the police before they got too busy (because criminals sleep in, right?), and reported four people breaking in. With that specific phrasing, my husband got more than he asked for with three police SUVs showing up within minutes. The six police officers were in full riot gear, ready to go. It was so intimidating, my husband confided that he thought he might "shit his pants", and realized he needed to step in. Quickly trying to de-escalate the situation, my husband informed the squad that it was a mother and three kids. The head officer dismissed the rest of the team and headed up to the unit. He was up there for hours with little to no results as she refused to leave, claiming squatter rights. Holding her position strong, she called in her friend as backup.

This event happened right after the George Floyd protests, when a 46-year-old black man died due to police brutality. All the police officers were on edge as they were more under the microscope than ever. So, after the squatter's friend arrived and whipped out her camera to film the situation, the police sergeant was called. The police sergeant was a short bald man who had a very positive demeanor that cut the tension of our standoff. We were amazed at how he handled the situation with such kindness and grace, but with a firm hand. See, this woman had been kicked out from multiple buildings on our street, and the police department knew her well. "I see you have some kiddos here, that is very unfortunate, however, you are here illegally, and if you refuse to leave, we will have to arrest ya," the police sergeant said in a chipper tone and a matter-of-fact smile. With that, they started helping move her stuff out of the building. After the all-day ordeal, she was finally out. When we inspected the trashed unit, we found a giant collection of locks, presented like trophies, from all the buildings she had broken into.

Our property manager was amazed at how we were able to get the squatter out, on our own, in one day. Unfortunately, our relationship with our manager continued to get worse as they neglected tenants, leaving emails and phone calls unanswered for two to three weeks. Parting ways, we knew we were the least of our property manager's worries. We were small fish with only 12 units while their other clients, who were also hemorrhaging money, had over 100 units in their portfolio.

The "Unhandy" Handywoman

After we fired our property manager, we quickly realized that we needed eyes on the property at all times as tenants broke out in "he said, she said" situations. For example, we had hired one of our tenants, Michelle, in unit number seven, to clean and maintain the hallways. She was falling behind on rent and wanted to see if we could help her make ends meet. Unfortunately, that went up in flames as she stopped cleaning without telling anyone. Michelle had become pregnant and did not want to clean but continued to collect over a month's worth of payments until we caught on. We continued to support Michelle in efforts to keep her housed but, unfortunately, she had abused our trust and left the communal space in disrepair with no thought of the other tenants.

Eileen, one of our tenant's "caretakers", alerted us to the problem and eagerly volunteered for the job of being our on-site eyes and ears, boasting of her skills as a handywoman. It seemed like a good enough arrangement. She would keep her eye on the property, maintain the peace and order, do some light yard work, as well as a couple of odd handyman jobs for a modest sum. We even ended up giving her a unit rent-free. We did not ask for references as most people in this area just put down their friends or family to vouch for them. Since she already frequented the building as a tenant's "caretaker", how bad could she be? We quickly came to realize her skills as a handywoman were greatly exaggerated. Armed with YouTube and a business credit card (yes, I know), she would tackle each problem with grand enthusiasm, only to cost us three times the amount we would have paid a repairman, with little to nothing accomplished. Looking back, I should have set up a Home Depot account where they could call me to preauthorize charges. Handing out business credit cards is almost always a bad idea.

An example of one of these tasks was when we asked her to remove debris from the basement. The previous owners had used the area under the building to store their old construction waste as well as two oversized water heaters, which they had replaced. We intentionally asked Eileen to hire someone to remove the water heaters as they were too big to simply carry through the basement doorway. The framing to the basement had been previously reinforced, making the doorway narrower by four inches, and no longer allowing these large commercial water heaters to fit through in one piece. Rather than hiring a few guys to disassemble the water heaters, she bought a heavy-duty chain, a couple of sledgehammers, and hired two men from Home Depot to do the job "her way".

When we got wind of what was going on, we intervened and asked how she was planning on moving two 630lb commercial water heaters out of the building. Eileen informed us she had spent the day trying to pummel the water heaters to a size that could be squeezed through the basement doors, with no success. Intrigued by this thought process, we asked how she was planning to remove the water heaters if she was successful in pummeling them down to a manageable size that could fit through the doorway. Eileen then told us her plan, painting an alarming picture for us. The two men she picked up were going to wrap a heavy metal chain around the water heater. The men would guide it out of the doorway as she towed it out of the building and around a tree from the attached U-Haul she rented with our credit card. Keep in mind, there wasn't a straight shot from the basement to the vehicle, and even if it did work, it would have most likely taken out a few supporting beams for the building, collapsing at least one or more units. Luckily, the plan had not worked as she found she could not make the water heaters skinnier with the brute force of a sledgehammer.

After asking Eileen to return all the unused equipment and spending hundreds of dollars on unneeded labor, we found out she kept the U-Haul for five extra days as a "personal" car on our credit card, running up a $1,300 bill. Furious, my husband drove six hours to the apartment complex to handle the situation. He also brought along his dad, who had over ten years' worth of experience in construction. They spent the next two days fixing the broken basement stairs that Eileen had destroyed the day before and systematically cutting the water heaters into fourths so that they could be safely removed from the building. My father-in-law took this opportunity to spread the word of God to our entire apartment building and any passerby who would listen.

Eileen was an opportunist. Armed with a business credit card, she would buy personal items on a regular basis and say she lost the receipt. She completely remodeled her unit on our dime, installing various sliding doors, fake stick-on marble flooring on top of our brand-new laminate flooring, and inflating a pool in the middle of her unit. As you can imagine, it was a complete disaster when we eventually had to turn her unit. Realizing we could set up an account with Home Depot to have receipts automatically emailed to us, we caught on, and shortly after canceled her credit card access.

Confessions of a Section 8 Landlord

Our handywoman had her own way of doing things. She was scared of weed wackers and refused to let us buy her one. Instead, she chose to use a machete as her own ghetto weed wacker. Terrified this was going to be a liability, my husband would try and hide her machete whenever he was in town, letting her know this wasn't a safe gardening method. We once caught Eileen cleaning her apartment floor by pouring two inches of water directly on the floor and dancing around her apartment barefoot with rags on her feet. Needless to say, we always knew when she was cleaning as we would get a call from the downstairs unit letting us know we had a leak in the ceiling. It also didn't help that she decided to install a horse trough in her unit to take baths in.

The building had numerous problems with squatters, so Eileen took it upon herself to keep the units safe by recruiting her friends to sleep on the floor of the vacant units until it was ready to be filled. Once finding a mouse in one of the units, rather than calling the pest control company, Eileen borrowed a cat from a friend to patrol the unit. We didn't allow pets of any kind in the building but decided to make an exception. Within one day, the pest problem was solved. "This is great!" I thought. "We just saved a few hundred dollars thanks to Eileen's out-of-the-box thinking." Little did we know that the cat was never returned. Instead, Eileen kept the cat in her unit under the kitchen sink. This cat used the cabinets as a litter box as Eileen kept it cooped up in there to hide the fact that she was harboring a pet in her unit. When we eventually had to turn that unit almost a year later, we had to rip out all the cabinets and subflooring due to the overwhelming stench of cat urine.

Eileen was good with people and was known as the building mom. All the tenants came to her for their problems. Every tenant had her personal number and would reach out for any problem, whether or not it was building-related. I had to keep reminding her to stop getting involved in tenants' personal lives as they often left her in pretty hot water. Once, she let us know that a tenant had called her, saying she ran out of gas and needed a ride. Little did she know that the tenant was trying to escape child protective services. This tenant had been caught with cocaine in her bloodstream at the hospital after giving birth, and child protective services was coming to remove her newborn baby. Not only did Eileen unwittingly aid in the initial escape from child protective services, but once escape was no longer an option, she volunteered to be a "co-parent" for the child so the baby could stay with her mom. I was blown away when I heard Eileen got approved as she was a functioning alcoholic.

Confessions of a Section 8 Landlord

My husband discovered this one morning when he had an hour to kill before an early morning inspection. He asked Eileen if he could treat her to a breakfast burrito while they waited. They each ordered burritos and large coffees at a local cafe. When they sat down, Eileen pulled out a quarter-pint of vodka. My husband initially didn't think too much of it, assuming she was going to spike her coffee with an ounce or so. Eileen made sure to offer some to my husband before pouring the whole quarter-pint into her coffee. Downing the entire vodka-flavored coffee within two hours, she confided this was how she started every day before 9 am.

Eileen did have a way with the tenants. She knew them all inside and out… and even without clothes. We referred to one of our tenants, Destiny, in unit number eight, as "the nudist" as she always answered the door topless or even completely naked on her days off, to the point that we expected it. When we had potential buyers look at the building, Eileen had to knock on Destiny's door first to give her notice to put some clothes on. Destiny was an aspiring stripper and had installed a stripper pole in her unit, which both her and Eileen would practice on.

Eileen would also inform us of all the gossip in the building, which is how we heard about the 200lb prostitute. We had a great tenant for over a year in unit number one, who was a beautiful black woman. We didn't know much about her besides that she was a bus driver until she was about to move out and buy a house. I was impressed and genuinely happy for her that she was able to save up and buy her own home with the modest income she brought in. When our tenant moved out, we found out that she was also a stripper with extracurriculars. Eileen, embarrassed, told me she found a large suitcase full to the brim with a various assortment of dildos. Horrified, she asked if she had to return it to the tenant or hold on to it for her. This, however, is not the juicy part. Right before she was about to move out, there was an incident that supposedly happened quite often, but this was the first time I learned about it. Our tenant's husband had a taste for large women, unlike his petite wife. He had a habit of hiring 200lb prostitutes while his wife was away, and stiffing on the bill. These prostitutes would later show up at odd hours, banging on the door to collect, and they continued to do so well after the couple had moved out.

    Our handywoman may have had her quirks, however, deep down, she was a good person, but not too good that she didn't fantasize about running away with my husband. Eileen had gotten it in her head that she and my husband had some sort of tryst. She made jokes about running away together. One day, Eileen called my husband saying she was going to drive to our city. My husband asked what plans she had in town. Eileen confided she was going to come out to see him. Setting clear boundaries, my husband said to have fun on her trip, but they were not meeting up. It got so bad near the end that she refused to speak with me directly, as in her mind, I was the other woman. I was not concerned... and if you ever saw her, you would know why.

You could tell Eileen used to be beautiful in her day, but the years of drugs and alcohol had taken their toll. She had an unhealthy dull gray complexion with a smile that displayed her various missing teeth. With her tall hunched figure, dressed entirely in black, constantly walking up and down the hallways, she was referred to as the Grim Reaper. She kept her hair tightly pulled back from her face, accentuating her gaunt features and large hoop earrings. She towered over most people with her six-foot stature, which was exaggerated by her platform combat boots. Between her stature and eerie looks, she came across as quite intimidating and even more so if you were not on her good side.

While our tenants loved Eileen, they were also scared of her. I remember her discussing once about how she could take care of a problematic tenant for us. "I know people who could take them out," she said. "We will just feed the body to the pigs.

No body, no crime." In shock at that statement, I laughed it off nervously. To this day, I still do not know if she was joking.

The Corrupt Politician

Not only was Eileen good with the tenants, knowing the ins and outs of the happenings in our building, but she was extremely well-connected within the community. She always knew the scoop of what was going on. This is mainly due to the fact that she also worked for one of the largest landlords in our city—the former council member, Rick Johnson. We felt a sense of ease knowing we had an in with one of the longest-standing council members.

Rick was part of the framework of this community. This silver-haired, 70-year-old black man had been involved in this city's political scene since he was 19, with the longest consecutive run of city council for 16 years. Every Friday, Rick had a standing meeting with the police chief at a local cafe, and knew everyone in his town. He had tried to run for Mayor in numerous elections but was yet to be elected. Eileen, knowing a good source of information when she sees one, would meet with Rick weekly and get his advice on some of the trickiest situations we encountered during the eviction moratorium. She would even stay in some of his vacant units when she needed a break from the other tenants.

We assumed that the former council member, a pillar of this community, would have owned much nicer properties than ours. However, that was not the case. There were areas of the city that looked like you were in a third-world country. The streets were lined with decrepit buildings that many would assume were vacant. Those were the type of buildings that Rick owned. A lot of his properties were previously motels that had haphazardly been converted into some sort of long-term housing. Curious, I looked up one of his "Motels" online to find some eye-opening reviews. Many people reported that the rooms were being rented out monthly with no kitchen or operable bathrooms. That the units were dirty, uninhabitable, with infestations of bed bugs, roaches, and mice. The city had enacted an ordinance that all residential units that were rented needed to be inspected at least once every five years to proactively avoid or eliminate housing that was deemed to be below the minimum housing code standards. The reason Rick kept his properties as a motel was the fact that hotels were exempt from this ordinance.

Rick consistently ran on a platform calling to end homelessness in his city. Though he went about it in his own way. He was known as being one of the biggest slumlords in town. Saying he was getting people off the streets but was placing them in unsanitary living conditions while lining his own pockets. Many of his buildings were known for having trouble with drug activity, so it was convenient that he also owned a bail bonds company if they ran into any trouble. After seeing how many times Rick ran for Mayor with no success, I asked Eileen why he kept running. She said he would run almost every year because he made a lot of money from fundraising for the campaign, insinuating that he pocketed all the campaign money. Rick had no actual intention of winning the election.

As we learned more and more about him through Eileen, we had to assume that some of the stories were fabricated as they were too outlandish to be true. However, many of these stories have been later confirmed to be a twisted reality. Eileen said that Rick was ready for anything as his beautiful home sported a massive underground bunker. He had transformed it into a skating rink at one time and rented it out to people wanting to try "residential skating". Rick had built up this beautiful home in the south side around the shambles of the neighborhood. People spoke about passing by it on the way to Walmart. It stuck out like a sore thumb and people in the community felt like it was a power move to show off his wealth and importance in this lower-income neighborhood.

During his time in office, Rick was known for privately funding an annual parade that would end at his house with a large BBQ feast. He had founded the city's Black Leadership Council, with the main focus of raising awareness and celebrating the Emancipation Proclamation Day that declared the freedom of slaves by throwing this annual parade. People recognized Rick by his large black pickup truck, which he would ride through the parade with his young wife by his side. This was one of the many events Rick put on without the city's support. He was referred to as corrupt and self-serving by the other politicians as Rick continued to get his way at every turn.

Rick was a not-so-successful boxer. To prop himself up, he funded a fundraiser where he was going to fight one of the greatest heavyweight boxers of all time. Rick won that fight after paying the famous boxer to lose in the ring. Wondering where this man made all his money to basically own this town, we asked Eileen, who casually told us that Rick made all his money by busing in women from Mexico for sex trafficking. His current handyman was his right-hand man and would load women on a party bus to cross the border. Eileen even showed us the party bus that still sits on one of Rick's properties when she was borrowing some tools. How an elected official could get into office with that type of background was mind-blowing.

The Hand-Me-Down Unit

Due to the Covid-19 eviction moratorium, many tenants felt invincible and would take this time as a free for all on rent, damages to personal property, and other illicit behavior. One tenant, Carlyn, in unit nine, was kicked off Section 8 (or so we thought) and did not pay rent for over six months. What really happened, we found out after firing our property manager and getting someone on site, was the tenant moved out but claimed she still lived there. Carlyn had given the unit to her son and his buddy as a placeholder while stating she still lived in the unit. We were unaware until the son's girlfriend got out of prison and started to cause trouble. The girlfriend randomly fired a gun in our complex, kicked numerous holes in the hallway drywall, and slashed a random tenant's tires. When Eileen got her tires slashed, she said, "Ghetto takes care of ghetto," but decided to take it one step further by tracking down and speaking to this boy's grandmother.

During this time, we had already tried to exhaust legal options but every eviction attorney office had stopped answering calls due to the eviction moratorium. All the law offices had a similar voicemail, "We are sorry to inform you that our offices will be closed until further notice due to the eviction moratorium." I even called a few law offices that specialize in tenant law by mistake, and would get a cold response of, "We don't work with you people, only tenants." After about the 20th call, we gave up pursuing any sort of legal recourse. There were absolutely no legal services available to landlords at this time.

The police were also no help as we needed to prove that the tenant was not living there. Every time the police were on their way, the boys got tipped off and called their mother to be there when the police arrived. Since there was no legal process we could follow and the boys were technically squatters, we decided to do a lockout when the boys left. We staked out the apartment and were ready to change the locks but found out they had been tipped off. When Eileen opened the door, there was a toddler in the unit, left unattended. They had borrowed someone else's kid so they would not get locked out while they were gone. To my surprise, this is actually a common thing to do when illegally holding a unit hostage.

Since the stakeout was a bust, we tried a more direct approach. When the boys were home the next day playing video games, Eileen banged on the door. Once it was open, she jammed her combat boot in the door and informed the boys that they were illegal squatters and needed to get out or the police would be called. They had a lot of expensive gaming equipment, as that's how they spent their days, and explained she would help them remove it so it wouldn't be stolen in the process. She escorted them out right then and there, helping them move their stuff. This was one of her finer moments as she talked the boys down, saying if they wanted to be men, they needed to step up and get a job. These boys later called my husband and apologized, then followed up by asking if they could rent another unit in the building after they got jobs.

Their mother, Carlyn, came running a few hours after the boys had been fully moved out to yell at Eileen as she felt entitled to the unit she had abandoned six months prior. This woman continued persistently to bang on her old unit's door for months even after we filled it, claiming that she lived there. She had a new Section 8 unit, however, believed she would be able to keep both units with the current political climate. More drama ensued when their mom eventually got the bill for all the past due rent. The boys came running with the bill. They were furious, saying they were going to burn down the building. We talked them down, but little did they know, it would be a godsend if the building did burn down.

The Handsy Handyman

Finally figuring out that our handywoman was not cut out for the job, we were introduced to a friend of Eileen's, Felix. He was dirt cheap and good at fixing odd jobs last minute. When my husband was in town, Eileen would tell Felix that while my husband was an attractive young man, that he is "the boss" and not to flirt with him (because he was hers, of course). Our handyman was a 70-year-old Hispanic man who had a 20-year-old male lover and would disappear for weeks taking part in massive orgies. He lived in a house across town that had multiple giant statues of Mary and an SUV that was spray-painted gold. I couldn't complain as he got us out of sticky situations numerous times, and as far as I was concerned, his extracurricular activities were his own business.

Felix saved our butts more times than I can count. One time, we were fixing some deferred maintenance, trying to repair a couple of small leaks in the basement plumbing. What started as a simple task became more complicated as it was directly tied to the water heater and we would have to shut off the water for the entire building while doing the work. Felix wasn't available, so we hired a local plumber that we had not worked with before. The plumber informed us it would be a quick and easy job. The first warning sign should have been that on his first attempt to fix the plumbing, he worked on the wrong pipe. When he came back the second time, I was later informed that he was intoxicated and was aggressively flirting with Michelle in unit number six, making her feel uncomfortable. The pipe he was supposed to fix was corroded. Rather than replacing the corroded pipe, he covered the leak with a watertight cloth and zip-tied it! Not only that, but he charged us as if he had replaced the pipe completely. He completed his work, turned on the water, and left.

Shortly after, I got a call while we were out on a walk with our toddler that the basement was flooded with two feet of water. The water had built up in the zip-tied section, causing the pipe to burst. In a panic, I gave the plumber a call and he said that, unfortunately, he could not make it back out until tomorrow. Knowing this is completely unacceptable to leave my tenants without water and an emergency-level leak, we called Felix. Luckily, Felix was no longer MIA and was able to get to the property asap, fix the problem, pump out the flooded basement, and set up fans so it wouldn't cause any mold. Anyone else would have taken hours and cost us a fortune at "emergency prices". I had no idea "emergency prices" were even a thing until that day. For those of you that don't know, if you need a plumber, electrician, you name it, right away due to an emergency situation, they will drop everything and come for two to three times their normal rate.

While our handyman was amazing at what he did, he had a habit of bringing his lover wherever he went. One day, while Felix was doing a repair, his lover, Seth, asked Eileen if he could use her apartment to make some soup as he wasn't feeling well. Agreeing, Eileen graciously set him up in her unit and left him to cook his soup. Unfortunately, this is where the story goes south. Seth was not actually making soup, but wax for dabbing. If you don't know what dabbing is, it is jargon that refers to inhaling vapors derived from marijuana. You create a wax, which a small portion is then heated with a blow torch, creating a vapor that is inhaled. When Eileen came back into her apartment to check on Seth, the draught from the door caused a grease fire. To make matters worse, Seth, in a panic, poured water on the fire, causing it to further ignite and blackening the ceiling and kitchen cabinets. Thinking fast, Eileen emptied a container of salt over the fire to contain it. Needless to say, that is the last time we had Felix and his lover back in our building.

The Scam Artist

Have you ever had a tenant move in where everything was an issue? Most property managers can spot them right away and will advise you to cut your losses and get them out as they will never be happy. Our tenant, Cindy, in unit two, would reach out every day with something new. The neighbors were too noisy in the middle of the day, the kids next door were playing in the hallway, there was a spider in her unit, or numerous small repairs needed to be done after she broke one thing after another in her unit. Every email she sent alluded to reporting us to some authority or taking legal action. We took care of everything to the best of our ability and in a timely fashion. Cindy was so difficult to work with that as soon as I saw her name in my inbox, my shoulders would tense up like the hackles of a dog.

Then, one day, her caseworker informed me that there was a serious case of black mold in her unit that ruined all her clothes and was causing my tenant and her baby health problems. My heart stopped in my chest—this was serious. Up until this point, none of her numerous complaints ever mentioned mold. Periodically, we would get notifications for mold throughout the year from tenants not properly ventilating the unit, which was an easy fix, but nothing this serious. We don't take mold lightly, so we hired a professional mold remediation company to go out the very next day. The mold remediator found no moisture when he used his tools to check for a leak behind the wall. He confirmed it was a ventilation problem from the tenant not opening her window. He treated the entire unit, and if any of you have done mold remediation, you know it is a very costly procedure. I had no problem paying the exorbitant cost if it meant we were able to fully clear the unit of all mold spores.

After getting a clean bill of health for the unit from the mold remediation company, we sent out educational information on how to properly ventilate one's unit to both our tenant, Cindy, and her caseworker. Like many small older apartments, the main ventilation source for our units was the bathroom window. We constantly had problems with tenants refusing to open the window when taking showers. This resulted in superficial mold in the bathroom, which is easily treated by bleach and replacing the drywall. Cindy's mold problem was much more pronounced, which left me scratching my head on how she accomplished this. Our educational information went over like a lead brick as Cindy claimed she was not at fault.

One week went by and I got an email from Cindy claiming the mold was back and the newly installed drywall was wet. Thinking there must be a leak that we missed, we checked the upstairs unit and resealed the roof but found nothing. We tried to get access right away to resolve the issues but was met with resistance from Cindy. She kept trying to restrict access. When we eventually were able to get in, demanding access due to the serious nature of the situation, we were met with opposition at every turn. Our vendor informed us that while he was trying to do the work on the drywall, Cindy demanded he work in the dark or pay for her utility bill for using her lights while he was in the unit.

While this was going on, we found out some suspicious information about our new tenant. We were informed that the tenant ran a hotel scam where the city paid for her to live in a hotel and the hotel took the credit card for incidentals. Somehow, she was able to falsely claim that she was charged twice and got a payout in the mail. I am not sure how she accomplished this. We learned about it when Cindy was boasting to other tenants that she scammed the hotel and was waving around her big reimbursement check. This didn't sit well with us, but we decided to give her the benefit of the doubt.

When we went to reinstall the drywall a second time, our vendor informed us that the unit was like a steam room when he arrived. Upon removing the drywall, he found it was wet from inside the unit but was bone dry behind the drywall. Cindy was running scalding showers with no one in them and refusing to open any windows. This was how she was heating the unit since she was not responsible for the water bill. She was also hinting ever since she moved in that she wanted compensation for all the minor things that she complained about. Now Cindy wanted a new wardrobe, compensation for her inconvenience while we did the work on the unit, to pay her utility bill for using her lights, and more. We found out she had done this before at her previous residence, and while she wasn't evicted, she most likely received cash for keys. Thinking she was going to get a payout, Cindy decided to try again but was caught red-handed.

After this incident, we made sure that all new tenants had the educational resources on how to ventilate their unit with their lease, and signed an addendum that they received this information. We also added an entire section related to mold prevention. In this section, new tenants would sign a statement to say that they understood that they needed to properly ventilate their unit when bathing, cooking, dishwashing, and cleaning, as well as allow air circulation regularly. We also required renters' insurance so they could make claims against their own insurance.

Subsidized Housing – The Good, The Bad, and The Ugly

With our entire apartment complex on some sort of subsidized housing, we were able to stay afloat during Covid as we always had the subsidized portion of the rent guaranteed, or so we thought. What we quickly realized is all housing programs are not created equal. During our almost three years of owning this building, we utilized Section 8 and a handful of other local housing agencies that received government funding to place tenants.

When we bought the building, we inherited four tenants from this small organization that covered 100% of the tenants' rent at above-market prices. "This is great," I thought. "We should get all the tenants on this program." Unfortunately, it was less of a subsidized program and more of a subletting situation. This one-man show formed a nonprofit that overcharged people who would not ordinarily get into housing and took a cut off the top by subletting the unit. We left it alone at first since they consistently paid on time and we didn't have to hassle any tenants for rent. However, all of his units caused drama.

For a long time, we had to have a hazard company come in and clean up from time to time as one of the units had a domestic violence situation and we would find blood in the upstairs hallway. We were unable to kick them out as no one would confirm which unit it was. All we knew was that it was on the second floor where most of this company's units were. This company would also switch out tenants without us knowing. Once, they moved in a family of five into one of the studio apartments they were subletting. Since these tenants didn't have enough space, they would create a fire hazard by using our back staircase to store all their stuff. The staircase was jammed full of kids' toys, a whole Christmas tree, garbage, and even a small charcoal barbecue, which they used on the wood stairs, burning holes through the wood when they dropped coals. We were unable to evict them during Covid. So, instead, we had to hire a junk removal company to throw the subletters' stuff away after many notices to remove the items.

We sent many letters to this small organization regarding the numerous lease violations but they did nothing. This backfired as once the company realized we would be unable to evict them, they stopped paying all together. The various subletters later told me that they were still making rent payments, however, the organization refused to pay us. This left us paying for a good chunk of the loan payment for the building out of our personal pockets, while living with my in-laws. We didn't want to remove all of the tenants as we barely had any more money to cover the loan, and renovating each of those units would be very costly.

Trying to find a creative solution, we had all the current subletters sign new lease agreements with us at the lower monthly rent that we were supposed to be receiving from the company subletting the units. This was a win-win for all involved as we were able to remove the organization from the equation by having direct leases with the subletters, and were able to provide them with lower monthly rent. After doing so, we sent a letter demanding the past due rent from the organization or we would report them. That week, we received a check for over $5,000. While that solved some of the unit problems, we still had a few tenants that refused to pay even after signing a new lease agreement.

Slowly but surely, we got each of the non-paying tenants out with some creative problem-solving. They made their displeasure known. One even stole our refrigerator from the second floor. Eileen saw this appliance robbery in progress but chose to do nothing. The culprit was a friend of hers and she wanted to make sure we didn't know where he moved. Eileen thought that if she didn't disclose this information or report the incident, he wouldn't be charged for the various months of missed rent and stolen property.

As we learned more about our lower-income tenants, we found that if you got on a Section 8 program, it was the epitome of "making it". If you were on Section 8 and were able to keep it, you were golden. To most of us, scraping by on Section 8 doesn't sound appealing, but in this community, it was ingrained in them from an early age, just as some of us were told we had to become doctors or lawyers by our parents. We found Section 8 tenants in this community were satisfied with where they were at in life. I even had a tenant who just got her baby taken away and get pregnant again, within less than two months, with the sole purpose of keeping her higher subsidy.

On the other hand, some of the other programs that were not permanent, gave us tenants with a little more motivation to improve their lives. One program, in particular, that focused on helping unhoused families gave our tenants a year or two to get back on their feet with the support of actively involved social workers. These programs showed more promise as the tenants were motivated to get their lives back on track. With these programs, we were able to see people housed that were previously on the street and shortly move them up into more permanent housing solutions. For example, I will never forget the single dad and his two daughters that moved in. They were previously living in a car before this housing organization helped them get an accepted lease agreement with our building. This family was so excited to move in. Our building welcomed them with open arms, and Eileen even baked them a cake. The father cried with joy when he received the keys as he now had a permanent place for both him and his two young daughters. They were our tenants for exactly one year before they were accepted into a program where they could move into a single-family home in a nicer neighborhood.

    This organization that found permanent housing for the homeless was my favorite. We had a great working relationship with Nancy, the head caseworker. And by the time we were ready to sell our building, we were known as one of the best landlords in the area. However, it didn't start out that way. When we were first introduced to this organization by Eileen, we had yet to turn a unit by ourselves without a professional property manager. Still in the early stages of getting to know Eileen, we gave her the task of fixing some small repairs, painting, and cleaning the unit before move-in day. Seems simple enough. Eileen said the work had been completed, so my husband made the six-hour trip to finally meet Eileen and Nancy in person.

The hallways of the building were just cleaned, but it was a wet, windy day and someone had left the building door open. Piles of leaves littered the hallway, and muddy footprints were tracked in before the floors were even dry. That was Nancy's first initial impression when walking into the building. My husband's face went red, already embarrassed as it was supposed to be in pristine condition before she arrived. It gets worse. When they entered the unit, there were broken blinds, a missing closet rod, and debris on the floor. Clearly frustrated, Nancy coached Eileen through what needed to be done. When Nancy went to open the bottom kitchen cabinets, Eileen abruptly said, "Don't open that!" Nancy jumped back, and with a fearful expression, asked, "Why?! What's in there?" Eileen, now embarrassed as well, explained that she kept a cat under there and had not cleaned it yet. The space had a cat bed and was absolutely disgusting. Nancy luckily didn't write us off then and there, and gave us another chance. The funny thing was, while coaching Eileen on how to repair the room, Nancy and Eileen became good friends.

Even with all the ups and downs, I still continue to take subsidized housing to this day as I found that people are people.

There are going to be good tenants and bad tenants whether they are on a subsidized housing program or not and should be screened as such. I also learned that Section 8 is not the only subsidized housing program. There are numerous options out there, and many are actually superior to Section 8. Some subsidized housing programs partner with landlords to help drive successful results, which, in turn, gives them access to more units. When we started working with Nancy, she made it clear that she wanted to fill all of our vacant units and requested that we inform her of any units that were opening up before we listed them. Looking back, the enormous amount of stress we endured seemed worth it as we were able to move roughly ten people out of homelessness and improve their lives during the three years we owned the building.

Robin Hood of the Street

As we were able to remove multiple unpaying tenants, we had a few vacant units that we needed to fill. We were told by Eileen that some of the applicants for our vacant units were fake as a local drug dealer, Dario, had gotten wind of the multiple vacancies. I had no idea what that meant at the time. She explained that while they looked great on paper, with stable jobs and excellent credit, they were being paid by a local drug dealer to move in and take control of the unit. The plan was to get accepted, move in, and immediately hand over the unit for a sizable fee to the drug dealer. He wanted to use the unit as a "trap house", which is a place to sell drugs. Since we were in the middle of an eviction moratorium due to Covid-19, there would be nothing we could do about it if they got in. We were worried about the legal ramifications of turning down these seemingly qualified tenants, however, we knew the nightmare that would ensue if people started selling drugs out of our building.

Once we started turning down fake applicants, Dario got a hold of my husband's phone number after harassing one of our tenants. You would think one would be shaking in their boots to get called by the top drug dealer in one of the most dangerous cities. However, six hours of distance can give you some extra unearned confidence. Dario's call started off very professionally, which caught us off guard.

"I am calling on behalf of Latrice and wanted to know why her application has not been approved," Dario stated almost as if he was the applicant's caseworker.

Taken aback, my husband replied, "Who is this?"

"This is Dario," he muttered and my husband instantly knew this was the person trying to turn our unit into a trap house. My husband knew this could not continue and put Dario in his place right then and there.

In an extremely aggressive tone, my husband replied, "I don't know how you got my number. If Latrice wants to give me a call, then she can give me a call. This has nothing to do with you. You have no business with my unit. Don't ever fucking call me again."

I had never heard him speak like that to anyone, and Dario never called back. However, it was a continuous problem. We never knew if an application was "fake" or not and had to use our best judgment. After many sleepless nights, we came up with a solution. We started to tell the suspected fake tenants that we were only leasing to Section 8 tenants, which seemed to mediate the problem. We even looked into hosting police officer meetings in our building's common area to make the space less attractive. A few weeks later, the problem resolved itself as Eileen informed us that the drug dealer was recently shot and killed and would no longer be an issue.

Little did we know that Dario was a big deal in the area and was beloved by the low-income community. He was a hardcore gangster, but he also gave back and supported many of the low-income families. This drug dealer was regarded as the Robin Hood of the hood. When he passed, the community threw him a large Mardi Gras-style parade down our street. He was missed by many, but needless to say, we rested a little bit easier.

Attack of the Roaches

Most of you may know that as a landlord, you expect to set aside roughly 30% of your total income towards maintenance. However, if you own an older building that mainly focuses on subsidizing hosting, expect to pay double that. Maintenance and upkeep was always a never-ending struggle as we tried to keep the building in the condition we bought it in. When we purchased the building, it had been recently flipped and the units had barely been filed. Since they were flipping the apartment complex, they didn't worry about thoroughly screening their tenants. They just filled it with bodies and sold it. Which gives you some insight on the quality of tenants we inherited.

One of the biggest issues we faced was roaches. If any of you have ever had an experience with an infestation of German roaches, which I refer to as "the small ones", you know they are almost impossible to get rid of. I always breathe a little easier after I get a complaint and see the large ones that you sometimes see come in from outside as they are easy to get rid of. But the small ones give me PTSD. I have personally experienced the nightmare of roaches in our first apartment that we could barely afford. We had roaches so bad that when you turned off the lights, you could hear them scurrying around. My brother, to this day, still recounts the tales of when he spent the night in my apartment. As soon as he turned off the lights, my apartment came alive with roaches coming out of the walls. We had the room treated a few times but the roaches would just retreat to another unit and come back full force after the poison had dissipated. What I later learned is the only way to get rid of these buggers is to treat the entire building at one time.

I immediately gave my landlord notice the day after one ran across my face while I was sleeping. A few days later, when I came back into the unit to collect my stuff, roaches rained down from the door frame as I entered my old apartment. Even after moving, they followed me in all my moving boxes, furniture, and electronics. We had to throw out a lot of infested furniture and electronics. The belongings we did keep had to be left and unpacked out on the driveway of our new home to mitigate the transfer of these disgusting pests. So, I understand first-hand how horrible it is to live with roaches.

When dealing with subsidized units, roaches were a constant problem. If you are finally able to get rid of these pests, they come right back again from the constant supply of infested used furniture, or one of the many items our tenants would pick up off the curb. I once found a box of donated food outside one of my tenant's units crawling with roaches. We were determined to win the battle against these little buggers. We had our units treated monthly as well as fumigated the entire building on multiple occasions. Unfortunately, we always had a few tenants that would refuse to give us access. The funny thing was, those were the units that would try and report us to the housing authority in order to not pay rent. Since we were doing everything in our power to remedy the situation and could present the detailed contract with our scheduled maintenance with a professional pest control company, we never received a citation.

While we avoided citations for the roaches, we did often get citations for the new city clean-up ordinances. In order to clean up the streets, the city passed an ordinance that would fine the building owners if tenants left their furniture, mattresses, or other various forms of garbage on the sidewalk. We constantly received fines after transients or even people from other buildings dumped their furniture in front of our apartment complex. After numerous fines and constant frustration on fixing the never-ending supply of old mattresses, I found a workaround. There is a number to call the city and report obstructed sidewalks. Not disclosing I was the landlord, I would call and report mattresses that were in the street or on the sidewalk next to our building. The city would send someone to come by and pick it up, which ended up saving us hundreds of dollars.

The other major problem was illegal dumping of trash from other building owners on the block. I even caught another building owner red-handed pouring his overflow trash into our dumpster, leaving our tenants no choice but to pile their garbage outside of the dumpster. The kicker was during Covid, the trash pickup service would routinely cancel pickup due to low staffing. We were left paying the same enormous garbage bill, and were being fined by the city when there was a pile-up. Unfortunately, this was an ongoing problem that we were unable to solve, but not for the lack of trying. We paid for a bar lock on our dumpster and gave each tenant a key. However, none of the tenants would lock it after they dumped their trash in, and of course, this would further set us back on our never-ending battle against the roaches.

Along with battling against the constant piles of trash and the roaches that came with them, our tenants found ways to mess with us. Once, after I sent out a chain of lease violation notices, an unknown tenant responded by shooting off the upstairs fire extinguisher in the hallway. Shortly after, they reported us to the fire department for not having an unused fire extinguisher on that floor.

One of the biggest repairs we had to perform on our building was replacing two 400-gallon water tanks. With one already out and the second about ready to go, we had to work fast in order to not leave our tenants without hot water. Everyone we spoke to wanted $10,000 to do the job, which we simply did not have the budget for at the time. We knew we were being overcharged as the contractors we spoke to made it clear they thought we had no other choice than paying the exorbitant fee. Thinking fast, we made other plans. We were able to assemble a crew of tradesmen from our hometown that we had worked with before, and bring them six hours away to our apartment complex to get the job done. Driving these men three hundred miles, housing, and feeding them for two days, plus paying them a fair wage cost us less than half of all the previous bids.

Some of our biggest lessons while managing this building was to find the most effective way to keep our building maintained while not breaking the bank. Between our battles with roaches, illegal dumping, and trying to keep up with our building maintenance, we had our hands full. Little steps like

Confessions of a Section 8 Landlord

calling the city to pick up mattresses or being resourceful with our maintenance saved us thousands of dollars and allowed us to keep the building during this precarious time.

The Gentle Giant

One of our tenants, Darius, in unit number two, was the unofficial security guard for the building. He was a 350lb black man who would like to sit out in front of the building. For the most part, he gave us no trouble and helped out around the apartment complex when he needed some extra cash. For example, when two grown men were struggling to move two 400lb water heaters out of the basement, he simply picked them up and asked where we wanted them without breaking a sweat. The local gang leaders were always trying to recruit him as their muscle but he had no interest in getting involved.

Over the years, he was a constant presence in our building. My husband even taught him how to drive one day when he was in town. Darius had recently purchased a brand-new car, which he guarded with his life. You could often find him fussing over his un-driven Scion XB outside our building. One day, while my husband was doing some work on the building, he saw Darius sitting by the steps crying, looking like someone killed his puppy. "What's the matter?" my husband asked. Darius explained that he just got his driver's permit and was supposed to have a driving lesson today but the person bailed at the last minute. So, my husband put down all his tools and took him for his first driving lesson to run an errand at the local bank.

Our gentle giant was not without faults. He was severely disabled and had the mental capacity of a seven-year-old. Eileen was supposedly his caretaker, however, to this day, I am still unsure of what she did, as whenever you entered his unit, there was an overwhelming smell of rotten food. The unit was always trashed with empty pizza boxes and expired food strewn about. I am pretty sure our roach problem stemmed from his unit as it was the most unhygienic thing I have ever seen. The biggest issue, however, was the massive crush he had on Eileen. Darius truly believed he was in a relationship with her. This became an issue as he would get jealous when Eileen went to grab a bite to eat with my husband. We had become the enemy before we knew it.

On the night right before we were doing a building inspection for some potential buyers, we got a call to find out our on-site person was in jail. "What the fuck!?" I blurted out at a friend's house as I tried to piece together what had happened. The day before, my husband had taken Eileen out to lunch to thank her for all the hard work she was doing. While she was out, Darius got more and more aggravated, thinking my husband stole his girlfriend. Eileen did not help the situation as it became clear to us that she led him on as she liked the attention.

When Eileen came back to the building to check on Darius, he was in a rage. Out of frustration, he broke his TV and dismantled the room. Fearful she was about to be rushed by this 350lb man, Eileen pulled a knife and gave him a warning cut on his forearm. When hearing the story, I envisioned his forearm completely cut open, gushing with blood, but when we saw him the next day, it looked like he had an aggressive papercut on his arm. Of course, the police were called and that landed her straight in jail along with all the keys for the building that we needed for tomorrow's inspection. "No worries," my husband said. He was simply going to bail her out. He called the police station and asked how he could place bail, assuming it was a couple of hundred dollars. We were informed that bail was set at $150,000. Well, that plan was clearly out. Instead, we had to brave the inspection with our agent, who flew up from our town, with absolutely no keys. During the inspection, there were no locksmiths available. Luckily, we were able to access 90% of the units. In order to get access, my husband crawled into some air shafts under the building to get into some units through the bathroom windows as the ventilation windows were interior facing.

Eileen was released a few days later and things continued to spiral. During the time she was being held in jail, Darius' sister was under the impression that Eileen stole personal property from her brother. She broke into Eileen's unit with a crowbar, completely destroying the door frame. When Eileen was released, she was furious at what had transpired. She informed us that she had her machete and no one would be breaking into her unit on her watch. Knowing that she had been baiting Darius on, I asked both of them to give each other space. However, no one could keep their twisted relationship apart.

One day, I heard that Eileen was in Darius' unit. Not wanting any more drama, I drew the line, stating that one of them had to go. Eileen calmly informed us that they had made amends. Darius had wandered up to her unit the other day complaining he was hungry, like a child coming to their mother. Eileen had made him two bags worth of chicken nuggets, and all was forgiven. This codependent relationship baffled me, but besides evicting one of them, which was still banned at the time, there was nothing I could do.

This hot and cold relationship between Darius and Eileen continued for some time. Every couple of months, our on-site person would disappear for a few days with no warning due to some medical emergency. After the incidents between her and Darius, we were unable to get ahold of her for almost a week and our tenants confirmed her car was still parked outside. Starting to get concerned, I asked my tenants if anyone had seen her leave the building, which they all confirmed they had not. Suspicious, I convinced one of our other on-site contacts to check out Darius' room to confirm she wasn't there. After no luck there, I asked them to check to see if there was a smell coming from our on-site person's room as I was concerned she might be dead in her unit. Right before I was about to call a locksmith to break into her room, I received a call that she was back from the hospital after having a medical emergency. I let out a huge sigh of relief that no one had died in my building on my watch.

The drama between Eileen and Darius continued to escalate to the point that cops were being called weekly for domestic disturbances. Sometimes Eileen or Darius would call the cops for something being stolen or the tenants would call due to loud shouting coming from one of their units. This became too much drama for us to bear and we had to ask Eileen to move out to keep some much-needed distance between her and the not-so-gentle giant.

Electrical Russian Roulette

During Covid, it seemed like a free for all with tenants trying anything they could not to pay their bills. Like most landlords, we got the run-of-the-mill refusal to pay rent due to Covid. However, the thing that tripped us up the most, and caused mountains of maintenance bills, was our electrical. We had started to have electrical problems where people were complaining that their bill was too high or only half of the electrical outlets in their unit were working. I didn't think too much of it at first as tenants had a habit of pulling massive amounts of power and blowing the fuse. We even caught a tenant running a long extension cord out of their window to power their friend's RV parked outside our building.

Not knowing what was going on, we hired numerous electricians until, one day a local handyman told us sometimes low-income tenants would go down and switch the wiring off their breaker so they would not have to pay for their electricity. We had two squatters at the time and recently had our basement broken into with a crowbar, which made the startling explanation seem plausible. After utilizing numerous electricians to no avail, I asked my dad, who worked as an electrician for many years, to come to the property with me. We went through each of the 12 units, checking every single outlet over the course of two days, tagging which breaker each outlet was currently assigned to. After much investigation, we found out that each unit was paying roughly for half of their electrical and half of another unit's electrical.

After the painful process of orchestrating power shut-offs and invasive investigations of each unit's electrical, we were eventually able to rewire the entire building. Unfortunately, we continued to have our basement broken into. Not only were my tenants trying to reconfigure the electrical panel, but we also had a handful of transients trying to make their home in our basement. The front gate to the building was locked but tenants would let their friends in by propping open the front gate, giving everyone in the community access to our building.

One transient loved our place and kept coming back. We later found out he was actually a family member of one of our tenants. Not only would this transient break into our basement with a crowbar, but he would also knock on the doors of tenants late at night asking for various items. He even assaulted a tenant once. Time and time again, we would call the police to remove him for trespassing. However, that was just a Band-Aid for the problem as the police simply would remove him and drop him a block away. Within a few days, he would be back and we would start the whole process over again.

I asked the police station how we could press charges so we could come up with a more permanent solution for the routine trespassing and property damage. They explained the only thing I could do was file a restraining order if I lived in the building. Since I did not personally live at the apartment complex, there was nothing I could do as a landlord unless I could convince another tenant to file a restraining order and go to court to enforce it. Since most of my tenants were not a fan of court, or police officers for that matter, it would be a non-starter.

One of our tenants took the situation into her own hands, without our knowledge. Using the tools at her disposal, she offered the transient a ride and spiked a drink she gave him with eye drops. Tetrahydrozoline, as I found out, is the chemical found in eye drops that constricts the blood vessels in the eyes, making them less red. This same chemical, if ingested, can slow the heart and one's breathing, which could lead to someone slipping into a coma. This knocked the transient out and she dropped him off in the next town. I was horrified when I found out—luckily, I was able to confirm he was, in fact, alive after the incident. Needless to say, we never had that problem again.

Keep in mind that this basement door wasn't flimsy. The door was metal with a metal mesh that should keep most people out. However, my tenants and the transients on our street were not most people. They came armed with crowbars, wire cutters, and a determination that, if put to good use, would really get them somewhere in life. In the end, we ended up buying a custom solid metal prison door for the basement. That was the best $2,000 I ever spent. While we slept better at night knowing we had a basically indestructible door, all the tenants who were previously breaking into the basement to mess with the electrical panel were outraged. I received numerous angry voicemails from tenants, furious that they could not get access to their electrical box. One tenant, in particular, called over and over again stating that she had a right to access her unit's electrical panel, and with that, we had figured out who was messing with the building's wiring.

The Dreaded Slip and Fall

Every landlord's worst nightmare is getting a slip-and-fall lawsuit on their hands. I have known a few landlords that stopped investing in real estate entirely due to how often they would get served with a slip-and-fall case. After the electrical debacle, Karen, in unit number five, demanded we pay her electric bill for the entire year. Since we knew there had been an issue with her unit, we were more than willing to compensate her. In order to fulfill her request, we asked her to send us copies of her electric bills. We needed these bills to not only confirm the amount we should send her but also to see when her electric bill had changed as we knew the issue was not present for the entire year. She outright refused, and the utility company could not provide us with the information as it was in her name.

After weeks of going back and forth requesting the necessary documents to release the funds, she texted me that if I do not do as she demanded and pay the full year without copies of the utility bills, she would seek other avenues of compensation. Frustrated as we had already agreed to compensate her, I just went ahead and paid her entire utility bill for the year, including her late and missed payment fees. I justified it as a way to sleep easier at night so I didn't have to worry about this looming problem. That was the worst decision I made while owning this building.

A few days later, we were informed that Karen had slipped on the small half-step in front of the building when she was coming back to her unit late at night after visiting her family in Ohio. She claimed that she had fractured her arm and wanted Eileen to sign a form saying she saw the incident, when, in reality, no one had been present. During this time, she never asked us for anything, just informed us while she gathered information for her case. When Eileen refused to sign the paperwork, Karen would harass her on a daily basis, banging on her door and yelling at Eileen to comply with her demands. Eileen let us know that Karen frequently banged on her window with the arm she allegedly hurt, which was currently wrapped in a sling.

Karen eventually sent us a document showing us that she went to the doctor to get x-rays; however, I am not sure she understood their findings, otherwise, she would not send us documentation that could later disapprove her case. The document stated that while she did, in fact, have evidence of a hairline fracture in her arm, it was apparent that it was from previous trauma. We never received a complaint from Karen directly, but soon after, we started receiving threatening letters from a personal injury attorney.

Never having been sued before, we were freaking out. I showed the letter we had received to an attorney and they advised us not to respond until we were actually served. Sometimes these sorts of issues resolve themselves as many of these personal injury attorneys are just fishing for low-hanging fruit without the intention of paying the fees to file a legal suit. These letters threatened that if we did not provide our insurance information, including our max deductible, they would pursue further legal action. They also requested all our video surveillance, which we did not have at the time. While we had some cameras installed at one time, the tenants would just get ladders, remove the cameras, and sell them for extra cash. We still had one camera up in non-working condition as a deterrent, but all the tenants knew it didn't work.

We continued to receive threatening letters from her attorneys for over a year with threat after threat going unanswered. Every new letter would say we had to respond by a certain date or they would pursue legal action. As date after date passed, nothing happened. Luckily, we hadn't made it easy for them as we were smart enough to hold our property in an LLC, which was owned by a holding company in Wyoming. This protected our identity and made it less worthwhile to pursue legal action.

Eventually, we sold the building and I received an angry text from Karen. She had received the notice from the new owners that they had bought the building and where to pay rent to. Fuming that she missed the opportunity to try to hurt us by holding up the sale, she tried a new angle stating we had to inform the tenants that the building was being sold 120 days before the sale's date. While this is true for residential homes, this is not the case for commercial buildings. Her last text before I blocked her number was, "See you in court, bitch". The very next day, we were served with the official lawsuit.

I was relieved that we had not responded to all those letters and were able to hold off getting served until we no longer owned the building. If we had been served before then, we would have had to disclose the lawsuit and most likely be unable to sell the building until it was resolved, which could have taken years. While our insurance covers the entire cost of this lawsuit without any deductibles, we still had to go through the stressful process of legal proceedings and depositions.

Our attorney, after reviewing all the facts, explained if this went to court, he was 99% sure we would win as it was a clear-cut nuisance case. However, he explained that most likely what would happen is the insurance company would settle outside of court as it is cheaper to do so. These personal injury attorneys know this and use many intimidation factors to make it seem like they are willing to go to court. And like a crystal ball, that is exactly what happened. Over a year and a half into the lawsuit, after the court date was set by our legal team, we received a letter informing us our insurance claim was closed as they settled the dispute for $37,500. The letter was bittersweet as while we were relieved that the legal issue was over, it was hard to come to terms with someone getting paid out for a false claim. Now we know that cases like these are a dime a dozen and, unfortunately, are just the cost of doing business.

Selling the Unsellable

Right as Covid hit, we decided we were done with the headaches of this building and were ready to list the property for sale. We started out hopeful we could unload the property in three months or less for a little bit more than we sold it for. Our main goal was just to break even. The one thing that really hurt us was our commercial loan. If you have ever had a commercial loan, you know they suck! You have a hefty down payment of 20%-35%. And while you can often get a 30-year amortized loan, they are normally ARM loans, which have to be refinanced every five years. This means that you continue to pay all the front-loaded interest time and time again.

I learned after this process to either stick with under five-unit residential loans, or get a better commercial loan with 16 or more units with the minimum loan amount of one million dollars. I was in the middle where commercial loans were hard to come by, so they had you by the balls. In the two and a half years we owned the building, 99.9% of our payments went to interest, so we had lowered our total loan amount by only a couple of thousand dollars. While we were able to raise all the rents in the building, substantially bringing up the value of the property, we were also hit with a 5% loan prepayment penalty. Not to mention the 6% on top of that we had to pay to our realtor. That is 11% we had to add on top of the original purchase price in order to break even.

We listed our building with a well-known broker in the area. They came in with all the bells and whistles with professional photos, drone footage, buyers packet, and listed the property on LoopNet. It was crickets for three months without a single offer. When I put some pressure on our broker, we got a few lowball offers but nothing that wouldn't be a loss for us. One of my friends, Trevor, was a commercial agent and sharp as a tack. He asked to see how my agent was promoting my building after my numerous complaints of no results. Taking a look, in seconds, Trevor poked so many holes in my agent's strategy that if it was a physical object, it would have looked like Swiss cheese. I will never forget when he said, "LoopNet is where deals go to die."

Knowing part of our problem was the price point, we decided to take it off the market, six months in, and gave it to the wholesaler we knew at a greatly reduced flat fee. In our mind, we could cut the 6% agent fee and reduce the price point to make the property more attractive. After doing this, we got an onslaught of potential buyers. "This is great," I thought. Who knew all we had to do was take it off the market. Unfortunately, most of these buyers were also undisclosed wholesalers trying to get the property under contract to reassign to another buyer. This resulted in inspection fatigue as we would get halfway through escrow, doing all the inspections, only to find the buyers could not perform. After a few months of wasting our time over and over again, I was about to give up.

I gave Trevor a call and explained my situation. He offered to take a crack at it, saying that he didn't mind flying up there for the inspection if we had a serious buyer in escrow. Knowing he was the man for the job, I gave him a shot even with the six-hour commute. Trevor had a completely different strategy from my first agent. He never placed it on the MLS, LoopNet, or other marketing sites. Keeping it as a pocket listing, he hit the phones, calling every landlord in the city to see if they wanted to purchase another building. The building had a lot of potential for a local investor and would have gone much smoother if we hadn't been six hours away. What we quickly learned is no investor with properties in the same city wanted to purchase on our street, except for city council member, Rick Johnson, who offered us three hundred thousand dollars under asking. Pivoting our strategy, Trevor started focusing on smaller landlords outside of the city who would like to trade up to a larger building.

Unlike my previous agent, who I spoke to every Friday with no news, Trevor never reached out unless he had something real. I had no idea until he brought me two winning offers that he had been diligently screening and dumping many offers he knew would not hold up in escrow. This relieved a lot of stress as I would get too invested in every offer, trying to see the light at the end of the tunnel from this nightmare of a property.

We finally got into escrow and Trevor came through on his promise to fly up to the property to be there for the inspection. He had heard the horror stories over the years and said, "I have never needed to bring my firearm to an inspection, but this might be the one." Trevor was a tall, well-built, bald, white man who would wear a suit to all his property inspections. Knowing that, to my tenants, he probably looked like a cop, we discussed leaving the suit at home. Even with the key debacle, with no access to the building keys due to Eileen being in jail at the time, Trevor handled the situation extremely well. He didn't take no for an answer and was able to access the unit as tenants tried to slam their doors in his face. Not only were we able to sell the building with Trevor's help, but we were able to get 11% over what we paid for it, and then some. When the building was sold, my husband said he could have kissed Trevor. Relaying this information, Trevor replied we could thank him by telling my husband not to kiss him.

We were immensely relieved to have finally been able to sell the building after it sat on the market for over a year. Our buyer purchased the building just as Covid relief efforts started to stabilize. While it felt like we had been to hell and back, aging us by 10 years due to the immense amount of stress, I wouldn't have done anything differently. As some would say, shit makes the best fertilizer. We had learned so much from the process that we were able to fine-tune our investment strategy, move our funds out of state in C class areas, and make incredible returns. Not only that, but we were able to successfully transition roughly 10 families from living on the streets to stable housing. I prided myself in the fact that even with all of the crazy stories, we were still considered one of the best landlords in the area by our housing partners.

Failing Up

They say failure is the key to success as it gives us the opportunity to truly learn from our mistakes. While we were fortunate enough not to lose our shirts during this experience, we did fail many, many times in various aspects of managing this highly volatile building. We learned numerous valuable lessons that you simply cannot go to school for. Trial by fire, they call it, and man were we on fire. Here are just some of the things we took from this experience that allowed us to fine-tune our investment strategy and provide much greater returns.

Location, Location, Location! You have heard it all before. Many investors choose to only focus on A or B class properties, which often is new construction in top-notch neighborhoods. I am simply not that person. While I would never recommend someone investing in an F class neighborhood riddled with crime and dilapidated buildings, I do feel there is a happy medium. With A class properties, you get all the security with little return like a savings account. Often, these properties won't have cash flow and the owners are hoping the properties will appreciate over time. I, however, have found a lot of success in C class neighborhoods, and enjoy helping low-income families find permanent housing solutions.

Even after everything I went through in this book, I still believe in subsidized housing programs. However, before investing in any area, I would highly recommend researching the health of the city, the jobs available, and the local crime rate. A great source for this information is other local investors on the real estate site, BiggerPockets, crime mapping websites, as well as checking out your city's economic development plan. And if an insurance provider ever turns you down due to the area of a building, don't walk... run away from the property!

I attribute a lot of our success from our first investment property to its close proximity. If you are just starting off on your investment journey, I highly recommend investing in a property that is less than an hour away. This will let you be more hands-on while you are learning the ropes. As you become more experienced, your proximity won't matter as much, as long as you have an experienced local property manager. Our 12-unit apartment complex wouldn't have been such a nightmare to manage if we had been closer to it or had an experienced property manager willing to take it on during the pandemic.

Another great resource to tell you about the area before you invest are property managers. Property managers will make or break you. I would always suggest you find a good one **before** you purchase a property in a new area. One of the things that took me a while to realize was how to manage a property manager. Even after this nightmare of a property, I continued to learn from the many property managers I worked with in Ohio and Indiana. Let's just say I wasn't the easiest person to work with at first, as I hired bad property manager after bad property manager.

While there are bad property managers, there is also a fine line between having a vision for your property and being one of those overbearing owners. The number one thing a property manager hates is dealing with an owner trying to do their job. That is why it is so important to screen property management companies thoroughly before hiring. You will be passing off your hard-earned investment to someone else, so you want to be able to thoroughly believe they can do their job without you constantly interfering.

The thing that drove me to fire my first property manager was the accounting. Make sure when you interview a property manager that you get a copy of their accounting and lease agreements. This way, you can see if you will be able to understand their books without having to harass them every month with explanations. I used to interview property managers with a long list of researched questions before my calls. Now I just ask to see their property management agreement, which will outline all their services and fees. Most property managers will charge roughly 10% a month of the gross rent but are willing to lower their rates as you get more units.

Whatever you do, don't just go looking for a property manager with the cheaper rates. Often, you get what you pay for. I would much rather pay a property manager more if it's going to save me hundreds of dollars due to an exceptional repair team or savvy lease policies. I found it's best not to pay too much attention to the monthly rate and focus more on all the additional fees and services, which will give a far greater picture. Those extra fees will bleed you dry if you're not careful.

Once you find a good property manager that you like and trust, hold on to them. Good property managers are like gold. I continue to invest mainly in one area due to it being in the radius served by my favorite property management team. Knowing I can be a lot, I make sure to keep my property manager happy. I make sure to refer them new business when I can. Also, a thoughtful Christmas gift goes a long way. I earned so much goodwill by just sending a box of See's Candies every year to my property managers. Property managers get the brunt of dealing with your tenants and a little appreciation can go a long way.

The other big question I get all the time is, "How do we get Section 8 tenants?" If you have a unit for rent in a low-income area, you will automatically start getting Section 8 applicants. Section 8 pays by the number of rooms. You can find out what Section 8 pays per room in your zip code through your area's Section 8 provider. When a Section 8 applicant applies, I screen them like any other tenant. Upon move-in, make sure all the occupants are on the Section 8 voucher. Section 8 does not allow additional occupants in the units, which could disqualify them from the program. The only big difference is that you will need to pass an initial inspection as well as comply with annual inspections and any repairs that come with them. If you fail the initial inspection, don't worry, they will give you a list of items that need to be repaired before the unit can be leased.

There are many things that can be removed from the unit that are not required for Section 8 and will keep you from doing ongoing repairs. For example, refrigerators are not required. Have your tenants provide. One of the most frequent complaints was from tenants overloading the refrigerator with food. This covered the vents, which caused the refrigerator to stop cooling properly. The other big one is closet doors. They are not required, and tenants almost always damage the doors or remove them completely. These will have to be fixed every year during the annual inspection. Other things to avoid are dishwashers, garbage disposals, ceiling fans, and screen doors. Go through and remove them all. This will keep you from costly repairs at every inspection.

Whether you have a single-family home or a large apartment complex, make sure to cap all the exterior water lines. If you don't, you will have tenants setting up pools in the yard, or even, God forbid, starting their own car wash business. If you do have a larger building with multiple units, make sure to properly secure the electrical box. We had to install a steel metal jail-style door on ours to keep people from rewiring the units. Last but not least, whenever you are about to have your annual Section 8 inspection, make sure to check your smoke detectors are still installed. It is common for tenants to remove the smoke detectors as they do not want to replace the batteries. If you want a more detailed account of what to remove or alter so that you almost always pass these inspections, I highly recommend the book, "Section 8 Bible" by Michael Mclean and Nick Cipriano. [1] This whole 186-page book is dedicated entirely to this subject matter.

Hopefully, after reading this book, you have learned a few things of what not to do, and know that even in the worst-case scenario, you can still pull through with almost any real estate investment. Investing in real estate is not like the stock market. Yes, you will have some good and bad years, but unlike the stock market, you own a physical asset that you can improve over time. Through raising the rents and/or adding value, you can force your property to appreciate even in the roughest of circumstances.

While we picked a horrible investment for our level of experience at the time, it taught me more than I could have ever imagined. Since then, we were able to flip a property in Dayton, Ohio. And now we have multiple out-of-state properties bringing in high cash flow ratios. Now we are able to sleep at night as the money comes in passively, with no management work on our end as we found an amazing property management team out of state.

In California, you often see a 3%-4% cap rate, which is the expected rate of return on your investment if your property was paid off in full. Out of state, in Indiana, we found a sweet spot in a C class neighborhood where we could get a 20% cap rate. We are able to get this cap rate by taking on a riskier investment while helping revitalize the community. One of the ways we help the community is by purchasing buildings that were previously uninhabitable and renovate them to Section 8 standards, helping increase the town's affordable housing supply.

This town has a lot of vacant homes due to the fact that it had been decimated when General Motors, who was the main job provider, went under. This caused a mass exodus, leaving vacant dilapidated buildings. As companies came in with new jobs and the city worked diligently on their economic development plan, investors started to revitalize the community for this new housing need. We would not have had the courage to go out of state and start exploring other markets like these if we hadn't gone through this experience managing a 12-unit building in an F class area.

Now many of our holdings have since doubled in value and we are able to take out all of our initial investment. This would give us an infinite cash-on-cash return since we would have no money left in the deal. Doing this allows us to invest and revitalize other homes in the community. Many people may look at this and say, "All you care about is money." Keep in mind, while I strive to be a responsible landlord by taking care of tenants and maintaining my buildings, this is an investment. We can't expect landlords to function at a loss, otherwise, they would just invest in the stock market rather than creating housing opportunities. Landlords prevent homelessness when they invest in creating housing solutions. The government knows this, which is why they encourage people to become real estate investors with tax incentives.

    Since our experience managing our apartment complex, not only did we have better skills to properly analyze potential deals, but we also had in the back of our minds, "How worse could it be?" We have been to hell and back and still live to tell the tale. This gave us the confidence to continue to try new things and take a few risks. Knowing what you know now, I encourage you to take the leap and see what you're made of. Investing in C class areas, as a responsible landlord, is a great way to give back to the community while securing your financial future. And if you're someone who fights for low-income tenants' rights, I applaud you and urge you to further help your cause by becoming a responsible landlord that creates housing solutions.

Epilogue – Giving Back
Permanent Housing Solutions

During the process of writing this book, I have worked with various housing advocacy groups to try and help fix the lack of low-income housing available while creating better pathways to permanent housing solutions. My experience in managing an apartment complex in one of the most dangerous cities in the United States condensed a lot of problems landlords see into a short period of time. This gave me some insight into the challenges that independent landlords face, as well as how many low-income families act/react in order to survive in this never-ending battle to stay in housing. My goal was to find win-win solutions that bring everyone to the table to discuss how we can create better pathways to permanent housing solutions.

I know there will be a lot of blowback from a landlord trying to resolve a problem that has been exacerbated since the 1980s with a background in large systemic issues. My goal is to take my perspective as a landlord and see if there is some common ground everyone can agree upon. I have been told that many of my solutions are in favor of the landlord. Yes, I agree, many of my solutions benefit landlords, but can't the solutions benefit both tenants and landlords? I truly believe there are win-win solutions for everyone. Why does someone have to lose for another to succeed? In the past, that's how it has been. Tenants have often lost while landlords have succeeded and, oftentimes, landlords have profited over tenants' misfortunes. However, it doesn't have to be that way.

I have seen first-hand what happens when new tenant laws have been implemented without a landlord buy-in. What starts off as something with the best of intentions ends up with disastrous results. For example, back in 2019, New York banned eviction records being used to screen tenants. Feeling backed in a corner, many landlords raised the credit score requirement to 700. This not only made it unlikely that their tenants had experienced an eviction, but it also made it harder for other applicants that had a clean eviction history to get into housing. One landlord I spoke to, who had over 50 Section 8 rentals, informed me that he used to give more leeway to his applicants; however, once New York restricted landlords to only charge one month's rent in a security deposit, he was no longer able to take on more risky applicants. We have seen a mass landlord exodus in New York. Due to the tightening restrictions, landlords sold off many of their single-family rentals to homeowners. While this may sound like a good thing, it did dramatically reduce the amount of rentals available, and due to the low supply, the cost of rent increased by roughly 30% in some counties.

Should landlords even be a part of this discussion? Some housing advocates have told me they don't believe that there should be any landlords and all rental housing should be provided by government or nonprofit agencies. While I disagree with that blanket statement, I do agree that certain groups would be best served by a service agency that is better equipped to handle the needs of the group. For example, in Andrew Hening's book, "So You Want to Solve Homelessness?", he describes how there are three distinct groups of people experiencing homelessness. [1]

First, there are people who need one-time financial assistance to get back on their feet. This would be for people that may have experienced a hardship that threw them off course, such as high cost of medical bills, divorce, or other life-altering events. Most of us can think of a time when an unforeseen event threw us off course and we had to lean on friends or family to get us back on track. What if you didn't have that support system in place? One of those unfortunate events could have put your housing status in question. Like many people you know, most of the unhoused community are very resilient and can get back into housing in a short period of time. One-time financial assistance, such as help with security deposit, could be all that is needed to overcome a hardship that got them off course.

The second group of people have been unhoused for a longer period of time and need assistance with Rapid Rehousing, which provides short to medium-term financial assistance paired with supportive services. This is very similar to the organization I worked with that helped single parents with children that were experiencing homelessness get housed. They offered support for the first year or two along with wrap-around services to help them succeed on their own after they "graduate" the program. This group could greatly benefit from landlords partnering with local nonprofits. Landlord partners could be a key part of this strategy when working with a landlord relationship manager. Having access to these units before they hit the open market could be the tool that many organizations need to secure housing for their clients.

The third group are people who are chronically homeless. They have been homeless for over a year and need permanent housing solutions as they are unable to be self-sufficient. These are the people we tend to think of when talking about the homeless. They are often talking to themselves on the street, living in their own filth, and creating public disturbances. This is the group of the most vulnerable people in our community, and they need to be able to have permanent housing solutions by a provider that can also provide the additional supportive services they need. I agree that this group would not be best served by small independent landlords as they need additional mental and physical care.

The other thing that I came across as I started this difficult conversation is the perception of who landlords are. I was told landlords are rich white men, or trust fund babies, and all they care about is money. We found that counter to popular belief, many small independent landlords do not fit this description. While I had an idea of who the demographic was that controlled most of the housing rental market, I wanted to put my theory to the test. After running the numbers, even I had some startling realizations.

While a lot of housing is controlled by large conglomerates—41%—almost half of rental units in the United States are owned by small "mom & pop" landlords. [2] This group of small independent landlords on average owns three properties and 45% manage their own properties. [3] Landlords have an average combined income of $97,000 a year, [4] and 31% of their income comes from their rental properties. [3] We often visualize landlords having piles of money with no care in the world besides how to collect their rent. The numbers confirmed my theory that a good chunk of landlords are small independent landlords that supplement their income with rental properties to keep up with the high cost of living.

What was shocking to me was that 44% of landlords are between the age of 18-34. [3] This is most likely due to the new trend of shared housing or "house hacking" as some call it. House hacking is where an individual will purchase a property with the intention of living there while renting out all the other rooms to lower their cost of living. We are also seeing very young landlords supplementing their income with little education on property management. Knowing this, we can create an education program that helps educate landlords on rules and regulations and supports them to become "good landlords".

What is a "good landlord"? Many people have their opinion on what makes a good landlord. In my humble opinion, a good landlord is someone with good intentions that is willing to change once they realize something they are doing is incorrect. A "good landlord" is responsive and proactive with maintenance requests. They keep the premises maintained and clean. A "good landlord" is willing to work with their tenants to come up with win-win solutions. They treat all tenants equally and strive to uphold all Fair Housing policies. As you can see, I stress the importance of intent. A large portion of these landlords are small independent landlords that are trying to navigate these complicated issues with very little background in property management. Having good intent is half the battle, and more often than not, there are a lot of landlords with good intentions that need a little extra guidance.

Many of these landlords get their advice and information from other investors they know, or from online resources. For example, Bigger Pockets is an online community, which is basically Facebook, LinkedIn for landlords. People go here to ask for advice and get answers to some of the problems they are facing. What positive change do you think we would see if there were educational resources for landlords through the local housing agencies. Think of how much of an impact that would make. While talking to other landlords can be helpful, they come from many different backgrounds and levels of experience. If we had an education platform with a well-defined standard process that was publicly available to landlords, I believe we would see immense positive change. Landlords could become certified through an education program with the incentive of having their units be prioritized for placement.

Confessions of a Section 8 Landlord

So, now that we have a better picture of who the landlord partners are and where they fit into the picture, let's talk about some ways landlords can help as well as how to get them on board with some of the solutions we are about to discuss.

One of the big issues we see when placing tenants is that many large property management companies use certain criteria to screen tenants that automatically removes most subsidized tenants from the applicant pool. Landlords need to make sure they have the same criteria for everyone as required by Fair Housing regulations. The big barriers to entry for many low-income tenants are the following standard criteria that have been adopted by most landlords:

- Verifying the applicants' income is 3x the monthly rent
- Credit Screening
- Background Checks
- Application Fee

During my research, I had the opportunity to watch the HUD Landlord Engagement and Unit Acquisition discussion, [5] which brought housing advocates, subsidized tenants, and landlords nationwide to discuss some of these issues and what had worked in their areas. A big component was getting rid of a lot of these "barriers to entry" and what it would take to get a landlord to agree to waive some or all these standard screenings so we can place more people in need of housing. The other big topic was how to get more landlords on board with accepting subsidized housing placements.

One thing that has been very effective is when subsidized housing programs have not only caseworkers but landlord relationship managers. This allows there to be an advocate for the tenants (the caseworkers) and an advocate for the landlords (the landlords relationship manager). Often, landlords do not like working with these programs as they can feel attacked or looked down upon by the caseworkers or other staff members. I myself have called organizations for help in finding a solution for one of my tenants and was told matter-of-factly that "we don't work for you people" in a tone that implied I was disgusting for just being a landlord. The issue is, not only do we all have our own set of biases on both sides, but we also use different language when we communicate.

When you have a landlord relationship manager who can develop a partnership with the participating landlords, often, the organization can get units before they even hit the open market. For example, one of the great subsidized housing programs I worked with had a landlord relationship manager that would touch base monthly to see if I had any units coming up where they could place tenants. This monthly call not only gave me the opportunity to pick her brain about problems we were having that developed rapport, but it also had me giving her almost all my units before they hit the market. This is a big win for landlords as they have someone that can help educate them on areas they may be lacking, and have units with placements ready, getting rid of the 4-6-week wait to find a new tenant.

    On reducing the "barriers to entry", one of the options that stood out the most and I have seen work in real-life situations is what they called a "one payment" system. Normally, when you have a Section 8 tenant, you receive a subsidized portion from Section 8 directly and the rest comes from the tenant. This often results in many late fees and evictions over small portions of rent that pile up over time. In some areas, they use a "one payment" system. This is where Section 8 or other subsidized programs provide the landlords with the full rent amount and the tenant pays their portion to Section 8 rather than the landlord. This is a win for the landlord as it saves them time tracking down the remaining rent and mountains of paperwork. It is also a win for the subsidizing program and tenant as it reduces the amount of late fees, the stress many tenants feel when they are short on rent and allows the program to get around two barriers to entry since they are supplying the full rent—there is no need for the 3x income qualification or credit check.

The other thing that is a hot topic right now are background checks. Alameda County in California has recently outlawed them all together for screening tenants. While I understand the reasoning behind it, landlords are terrified of this screening tool being taken away. The biggest things landlords are looking for besides eviction history is screening for violent crimes, domestic violence, pedophiles, and gang or drug-related crimes. While everyone needs housing, it is also the landlords' responsibility to keep their buildings safe for other tenants as well. If a landlord has too many incidents where the police are called or has been reported having drug activity in their building, they can face large monetary fines and potentially legal action. They could also lose great long-term tenants if they don't keep the space safe and family friendly.

So, how do we get landlords to waive background checks voluntarily? When there are strong partnerships between landlord and landlord relationship managers, you can often get around this by discussing what hard stop limit landlords have. Caseworkers know their clients and their backgrounds. Passing along this information to the landlord relationship manager, they can help place tenants based on coming up with a mutual agreement with the landlord partners regarding what criminal backgrounds would and would not be allowed.

These are ideas and solutions that I have discussed with my fellow investors. All who agreed that if we could tackle this problem with a partnership approach, we could solve so many of our housing problems. Too often, we come at this problem with an us versus them mentality, which closes off so many potential partnerships. We all want to solve many of these issues. While you may not agree with my point of view, I hope this at least starts a dialogue. Maybe even with someone on the other side of these issues from you. Where there is common ground, we can build. Build win-win solutions that will help bring more people together and into housing.

Sources

The Beginning of the End

1. Kiyosaki, Robert T. *Rich Dad Poor Dad*. New Delhi: Manjul Publishing House, 2020.

Case of the Disappearing Manager

2. Desmond, Matthew. *Evicted: Poverty and Profit in the American City*. New York: Crown Publishers, 2016.

Failing Up

3. Cipriano, Nick, and Michael McLean. *Section 8 Bible*. M. McLean, 2007.

Epilogue - Giving Back

4. Hening, Andrew. *So You Want to Solve Homelessness? Start Here*, 2022.
5. JPMorgan Chase & Co. "How did landlords fare during COVID?" Accessed May 4,

2023.https://www.jpmorganchase.com/institute/research/household-debt/how-did-landlords-fare-during-covid

6. Tenant Screening | TransUnion SmartMove | Tenant Background Check."TransUnion Research on Landlord Characteristics [Infographic] Smartmove|." Accessed May 4, 2023.https://www.mysmartmove.com/SmartMove/blog/todays-landlord-characteristics-infographic.page

7. Guzman, Gloria. "U.S. Median Household Income Up in 2018 From 2017." United States Census Bureau, Accessed May 4, 2023. https://www.census.gov/library/stories/2019/09/us-median-household-income-up-in-2018-from-2017.html

8. HUD Exchange. "Rapid Rehousing Roundtable Discussion Series: Landlord Engagement and Unit Acquisition – Part 1." Accessed May 4, 2023. https://www.hudexchange.info/trainings/courses/rapid-rehousing-roundtable-discussion-series-landlord-engagement-and-unit-acquisition/